Graveyards And Gardens

poems by

Marybeth Cohowicz

Finishing Line Press
Georgetown, Kentucky

Graveyards
And Gardens

Copyright © 2020 by Marybeth Cohowicz
ISBN 978-1-64662-169-9 First Edition
All rights reserved under International and Pan-American Copyright Conventions. No part of this book may be reproduced in any manner whatsoever without written permission from the publisher, except in the case of brief quotations embodied in critical articles and reviews.

ACKNOWLEDGMENTS

To all who have encouraged me
you changed the posture of my words
they stand a little taller
more confident
like they belong upon the page.

Publisher: Leah Maines
Editor: Christen Kincaid
Cover Art: Marybeth Cohowicz
Author Photo: Lorien Sanchez
Cover Design: Elizabeth Maines McCleavy

Printed in the USA on acid-free paper.
Order online: www.finishinglinepress.com
 also available on amazon.com

Author inquiries and mail orders:
Finishing Line Press
P. O. Box 1626
Georgetown, Kentucky 40324
U. S. A.

Table of Contents

I.	my heart cycles through	1
II.	we never stumble	2
III.	when planting a garden	3
IV.	my mouth	4
V.	the house inhales	5
VI.	pain and sadness	6
VII.	I watched	7
VIII.	the way you've broke me	8
IX.	the Wild in me is starving	9
X.	I scatter my	10
XI.	a dead bird's song	11
XII.	loving so hard	12
XIII.	Directions Home:	13
XIV.	I wished the sky	14
XV.	a moment born	15
XVI.	moonflower	16
XVII.	Death	17
XVIII.	some days	18
XIX.	we are all	19
XX.	falling all around you	20
XXI.	I pray for rain	21
XXII.	I could walk in the rain	22
XXIII.	to unlove	23
XXIV.	these words do not have	24
XXV.	nothing in me	25
XXVI.	a crown	26

To the survivors of Sadness and Sorrow, to those who have thrown them over their shoulder, and walk with a limp. To those who have buckled under their weight and the walk became too long. May a garden bloom in your wake.

I.

my chest cycles through
graveyard and garden as

my heart grows and dies
and grows and dies, but

at least there are always flowers
either way.

II.

we never stumble

where the earth is soft

welcoming

catching our bodies

like freshly dug graves

we stumble

walking over forgiveness

heartache, sorrow

all the places that

will bruise our bones

III.
      previously published in Heron Clan V anthology,
      Katherine James Books, 2018

when planting a garden

  push your finger gently
into an open wound
(that's the most fertile)

choose the seeds that weep
the most
     they are self-watering

  i like to use the ones from childhood
always having
so much luck with them   blooming into
all the shades of a freshly given bruise

     space about 3 breakdowns apart

  be sure to top the seeds with bullshit
i find a mixed bag of
guilt, regret, and blame in equal measure works best
   (if you can endure the putrid smell of decay it leaves on your conscience)
      it may take decades to manifest

  But

      Anything about me

        that is beautiful
      has been grown
        in the soil of sorrow.

IV.

my mouth
full of seeds that will
never grow, though my chest
so fertile

with the remains of
everything that has died
there, I haven't any tears
left to water them, I remember

a time
when there were so many
flowers I couldn't even
speak, but I can't cry

like that anymore

V.

the house inhales
lace curtains
blow in
it knows emptiness
and aches the same
as i.

the air in here
feels different
like it knows that
it will never kiss your skin again
we sit together in heavy silence
the air and i

as i count
Time
in breaths
and lives by
the deaths of my heart
and learning

i'm eternities old
and there's a thousand ways to die.

VI.

pain and sadness
is just a tilling of the dirt
to make more beautiful things grow

i am so fertile now
and ready for
a forest to break through
my bones

VII.

I watched

as a tractor   dragged   a tiller
across a field to prepare the earth

to be seeded, how I need that
to pass over me, a few times

I need to be prepared like earth,
            torn up
                  harrowed

my growing season is coming near

VIII.

the way you've broken me
only leaves cracks
for more beautiful things
to take root

I sit, waiting to become wild

IX.

the Wild in me is starving

feed me
your sky, let sunsets die
on my lips.

feed me
the midnight air and moonlight
that dances down your neck

the Wild in me is starving

hold your hand out
and feed me the Sadness
you've ripped from the garden
in my chest

X.

I scatter my
sadness and sorrows
by the handful

to the birds
they peck and peck
I want to tell them not to eat it

or they'll forget how to fly too

XI.

a dead bird's song
dies with him
all the air can do

is wait
for another bird
to become

happy or sad enough
to sing
the air doesn't care about

your feelings
it just doesn't want to be empty
for too long

some people are like the air
waiting for the next bird

XII.

*previously published in Heron Clan V anthology,
Katherine James Books, 2018*

loving so hard
we fall apart
but we were never meant

to stay whole
we were born
with cracks

and destined to break
in each other's hands, now
you're tangled in my ribs

and there is no
separating you from
bone or soul

XIII.

Directions Home:

turn at the corner where the trees
are blooming pink and white, and
the scent of lilac floats like a
secret on the air

go past the open field where
wildflowers worship at the feet of
the sunset

I'll be the girl dancing with the
moonlight

and you'll be home.

XIV.

I wished the sky

        smaller

I begged the stars

Reach your hands out

        for each other

Pull,   harder

Harder.   Until we share breath

Until we collide

XV.

a moment born
in between breaths
of a summer's night

this was not our lifetime

we were only meant
to collide
and leave a little bit of ourselves

on the other

but
I can still taste you
when the moonlight touches my lips

XVI.

moonflower
waiting on midnight
and I, for your lips

we bloom

XVII.

Death

kisses us on the cheek
right before we are born
and whispers I will see you again

Death

is our mother, never truly ready
to let her children go
we will always find our way back into her womb

XVIII.

some days
the smell of rich earth
reminds me of death and decay
but today I choose to believe
it is of rebirth
I will sink into this earth
bury my sorrows
within me are the seeds of sadness
waiting for Day Lilies
to burst open,
for hope to bloom in June

XIX.

we are all
a little weary

we all need to die
at least once

in our lifetime
and lay our sadness

to rest
I still hurt,

do not unearth me yet

XX.

falling all around you

like wild hair
on bare shoulders

summer rain
on kissing lovers

like silence falls
on a heart finally healed

XXI.

I pray for rain

and instead

the wind kisses my neck

the sun lays its head

on my shoulder

sometimes not even I

know I what need

XXII.

I could walk in the rain
all day long

and still never know
how a thirsty flower feels

but I know how it feels
to be wilted, I know how it feels

to want to rot in the earth

XXIII.

to unlove

like trying to place
raindrops
back in the sky

to unlove

is to defy gravity
change direction of flow

we are only meant to fall

XXIV.

these words do not have
soft silky petals, or

strong roots. They know not
the warmth of the sun. Yet

they grow inside me, ugly
and wild

XXV.

nothing in me
grows anymore
only you, you
vining around my bones
choking the red from blood
until it becomes
white as the moon

XXVI.

a crown
made of white washed

bone, tossed to the foot
of a rusty throne. Time,

like liquid
has changed its flow

you are my king
no more

Marybeth Cohowicz was born in Scranton, Pennsylvania in October of 1973 and shares her birthday with her beloved mother. Her mother and father were both textile factory workers. She was first introduced to Death on the day of her birth when doctors believed her to be stillborn, but diligently revived her.

During her lifetime she experienced many hardships. Living with an abusive alcoholic father, witnessing her mother struggle to raise two children in poverty upon leaving him, the death of many loved ones, sexual assault, and her own divorce are the cornerstones of her writing. However, she became an alchemist and turned her sorrow into gold. There is a line in one of her poems, "anything beautiful about me has been grown in the soil of sorrow". That has become the hallmark of her life. She draws a deep appreciation for simple joys, each one a flower in her "garden" of life, and has proven to shape her into a more compassionate human being.

For Marybeth, writing poetry began as a method of pain management to cope with emotions she otherwise felt unable to express. Her understanding of the human condition and ability to convey it in simple sincerity in her poetry has proven to be a great source of her own healing as well as for those who read it.

Marybeth Cohowicz has had numerous haiku published in Haiku Journal and Three Line Poetry and was named "One of Poetry's Best Kept Secrets" by online publication Bunbury magazine. She has had five poems published in Poems from the Heron Clan V, an anthology published by Katherine James Books, 2018, and one published in volume VI of the same, published in 2019.

She holds bachelor degrees in both Sociology and Criminal Justice, is a Marine Corps veteran, and works in K-12 education. Marybeth is currently residing in Michigan with her husband and four children where she enjoys sketching, and finds solace as an amateur photographer. Some of her photos can be found in poetry journals *Barren Magazine* and *Ink in Thirds*, and have also been featured in *MLive* media and the Ann Arbor news.

www.ingramcontent.com/pod-product-compliance
Lightning Source LLC
LaVergne TN
LVHW041512070426
835507LV00012B/1506